dow
CH

SPANISH-ENGLISH
Picture Dictionary

Catherine Bruzzone and Louise Millar

Illustrations by Louise Comfort and Steph Dix
Spanish adviser: Diego Blasco Vázquez

b small publishing

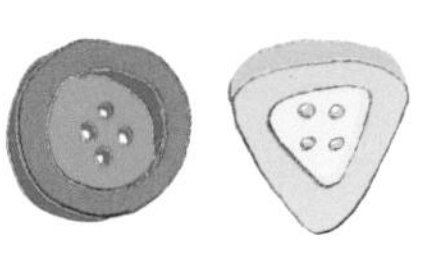

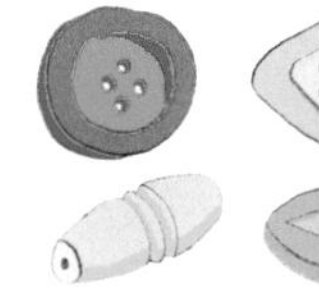

1 one
uno/una
oono/oona

2 two
dos
doss

3 three
tres
trayss

4 four
cuatro
kwa-tro

5 five
cinco
thin-ko

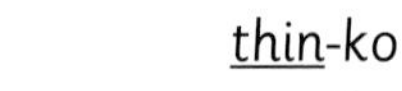

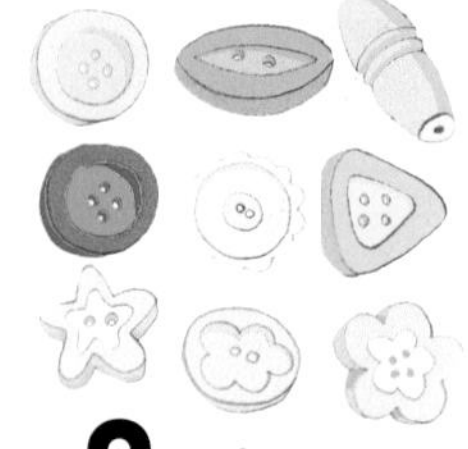

6 six
seis
sayss

7 seven
siete
see-eh-teh

8 eight
ocho
och-o

9 nine
nueve
noo-eh-beh

10 ten
diez
dee-ess

11
eleven
once
on-theh

12
twelve
doce
doth-eh

13
thirteen
trece
treth-eh

14
fourteen
catorce
kat-or-theh

15
fifteen
quince
kin-theh

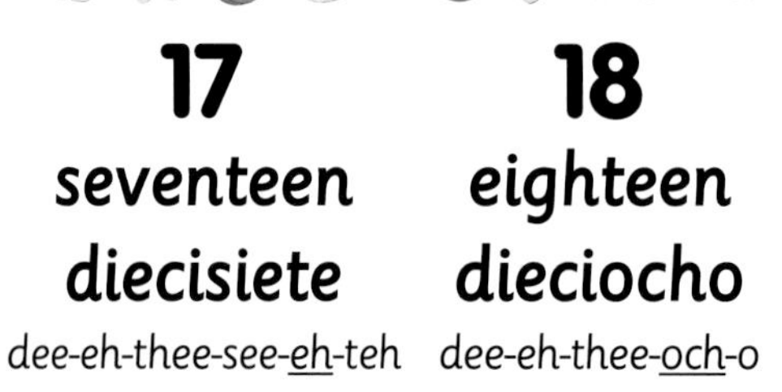

16
sixteen
dieciséis
dee-eh-thee-sayss

17
seventeen
diecisiete
dee-eh-thee-see-eh-teh

18
eighteen
dieciocho
dee-eh-thee-och-o

19
nineteen
diecinueve
dee-eh-thee-noo-eh-beh

20
twenty
veinte
vayn-teh

Contents – Sumario

soo-mah-reeyo

The body – El cuerpo

el koo-air-po

head
la cabeza
la kabeh-tha

eyes
los ojos
los oh-hos

nose
la nariz
lah nareeth

mouth
la boca
lah bokka

shoulders
los hombros
los ombros

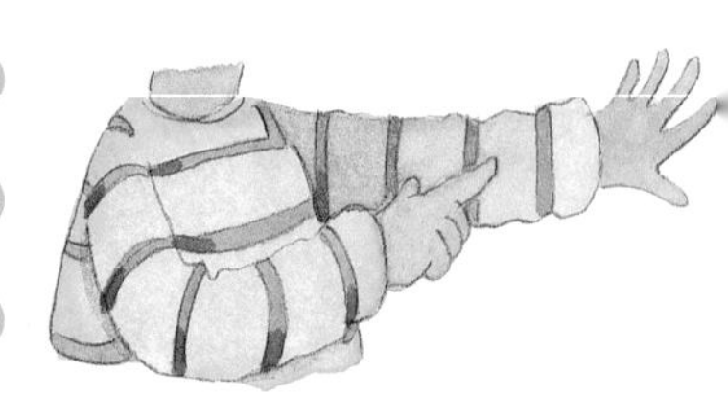

arm
el brazo
el brah-tho

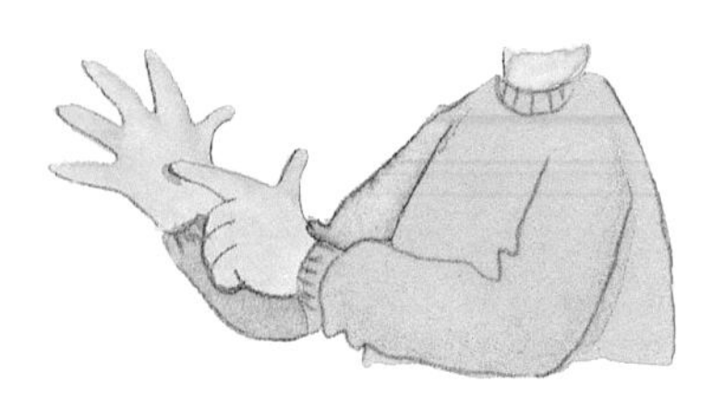

hand
la mano
lah mah-no

leg
la pierna
lah pee-yairna

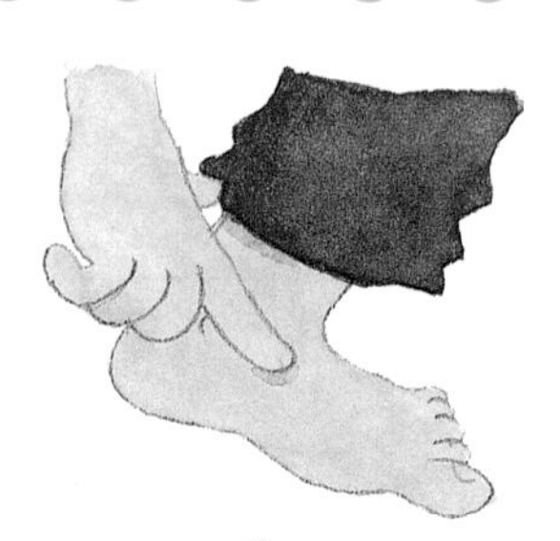

foot
el pie
el pee-yeh

Clothes – La ropa

lah roh-pa

skirt
la falda
lah falda

dress
el vestido
el besteedo

trousers
el pantalón
el pantalon

coat
el abrigo
el abree-go

shirt
la camisa
lah kah-mee-sa

pyjamas
el pijama
el peehah-ma

shoes
los zapatos
los thapat-toss

socks
los calcetines
los kaltheh-tee-ness

hat
el sombrero
el sombrairo

The family – La familia

lah fam-eel-ya

mother/Mummy
la madre/mamá
lah mah-dreh/mama

father/Daddy
el padre/papá
el pah-dreh/papa

sister
la hermana
lah airmah-na

brother
el hermano
el airmah-no

grandmother
la abuela
lah abweh-la

grandfather
el abuelo
el abweh-lo

aunt
la tía
lah tee-ya

uncle
el tío
el tee-yo

cousins
los primos
los pree-moss

The house – La casa

lah kah-za

kitchen
la cocina
lah kotheena

sitting room
el salón
el sal-on

bedroom
la habitación
lah abeeta-thee-yon

bathroom
el cuarto de baño
el kwar-to deh ban-yo

toilet
el váter
el bah-tair

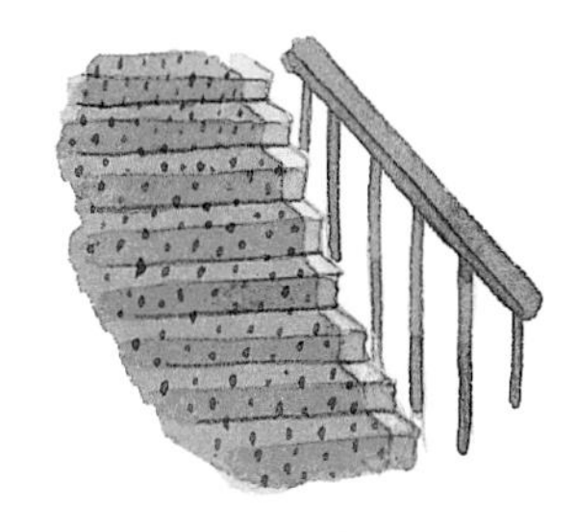

stairs
las escaleras
las eskal-airass

floor
el suelo
el sweh-lo

ceiling
el techo
el teh-cho

garden
el jardín
el hardeen

In the house – En la casa

en lah kah-za

sofa
el sofá
el soh-fa

armchair
el sillón
el seelon

cushion
el cojín
el koheen

curtains
las cortinas
lass kor-teen-ass

picture
el cuadro
el kwah-dro

stool
el taburete
el taboo-reh-teh

telephone
el teléfono
el teh-leh-fono

computer
el ordenador
el ordenad-dor

television
la televisión
lah teh-lehveezee-on

The kitchen – La cocina

lah kotheena

sink
el fregadero
el fregga-dair-o

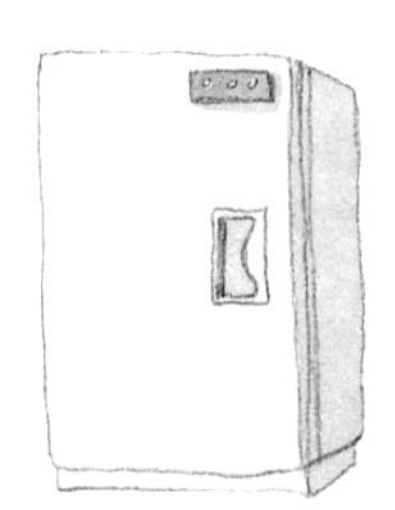

fridge
el frigorífico
el freegoree-feeko

cooker
la cocina
lah kotheena

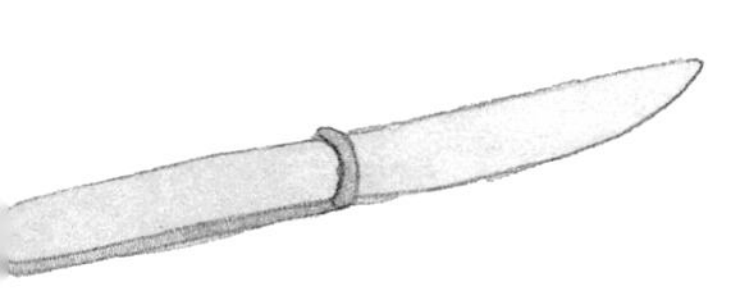

knife
el cuchillo
el koochee-yo

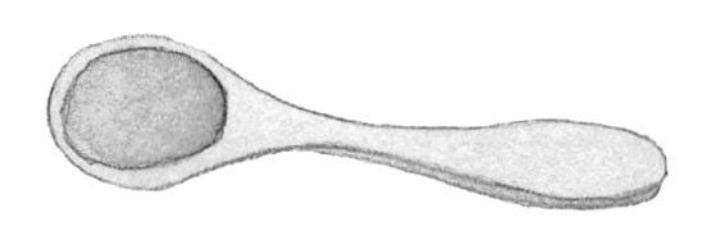

spoon
la cuchara
lah koochah-ra

fork
el tenedor
el teneh-dor

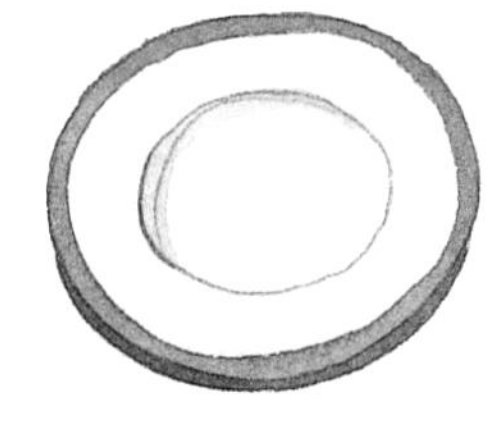

plate
el plato
el plah-to

glass
el vaso
el bah-so

saucepan
la cacerola
la katheh-roh-la

The bedroom – La habitación

lah abeeta-thee-yon

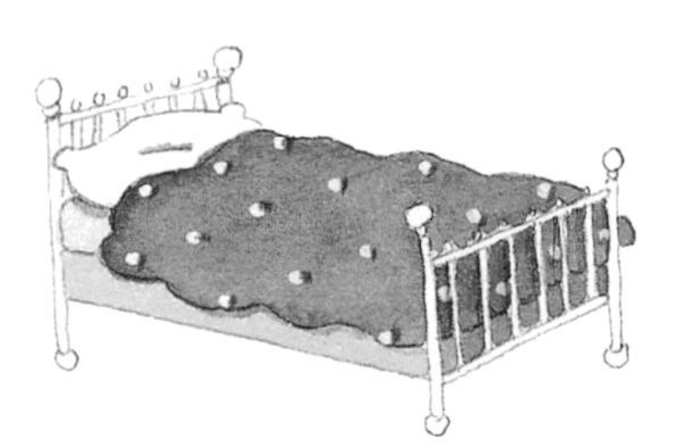

bed
la cama
lah kah-ma

chest of drawers
la cómoda
lah kom-oda

wardrobe
el armario
el ar-mah-reeyo

alarm clock
el despertador
el despairta-dor

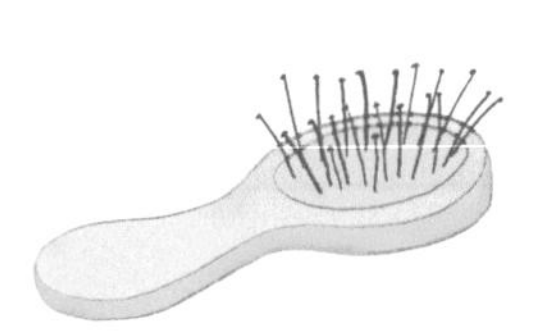

hairbrush
el cepillo del pelo
el thepee-yo del peh-lo

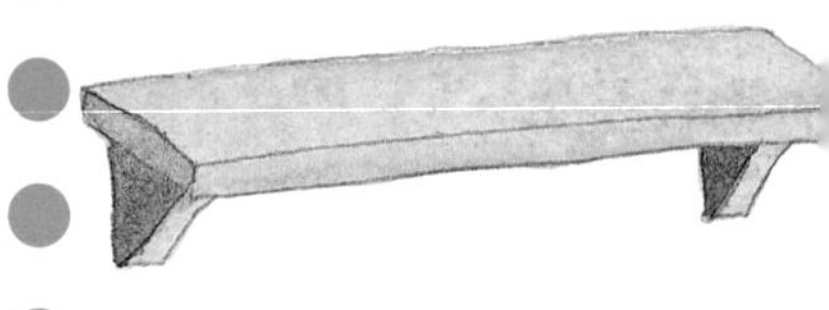

shelf
el estante
el est-anteh

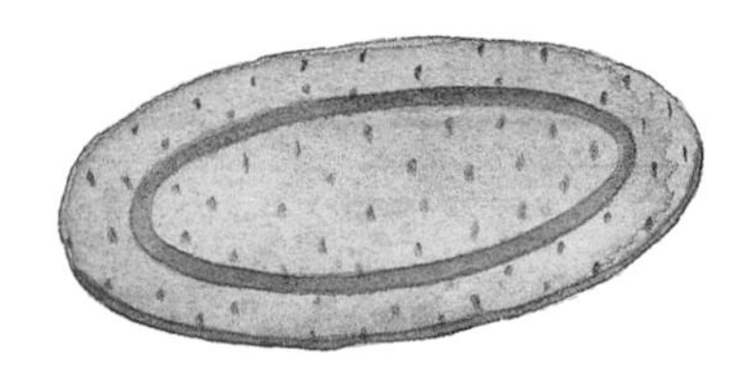

rug
la alfombra
lah al-fom-bra

window
la ventana
lah bentah-na

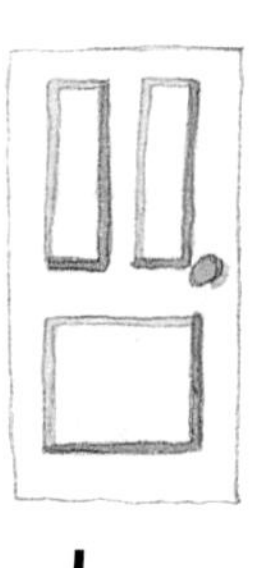

door
la puerta
lah pwairta

The bathroom – El cuarto de baño

el koo-ar-to der ban-yo

washbasin
el lavabo
el labah-bo

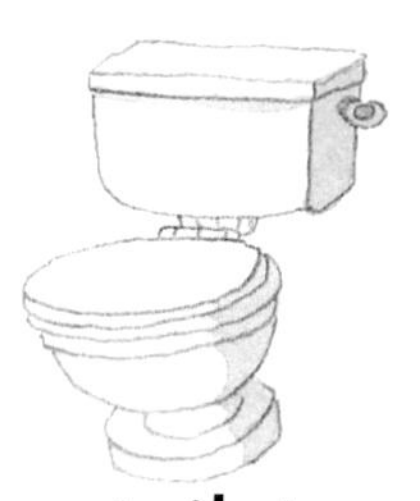

toilet
el váter
el bah-tair

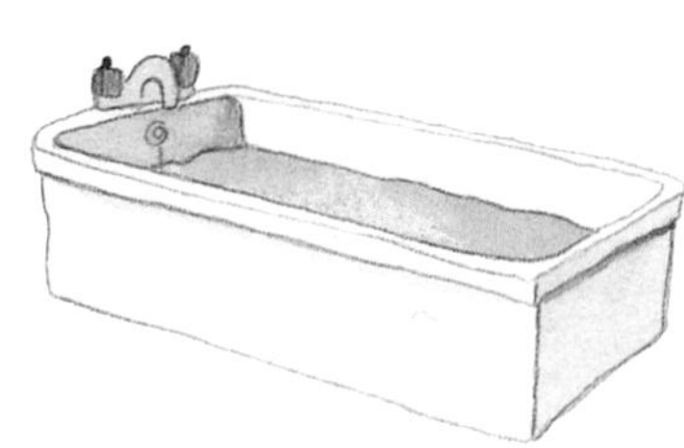

bath
la bañera
lah banyair-a

shower
la ducha
lah doocha

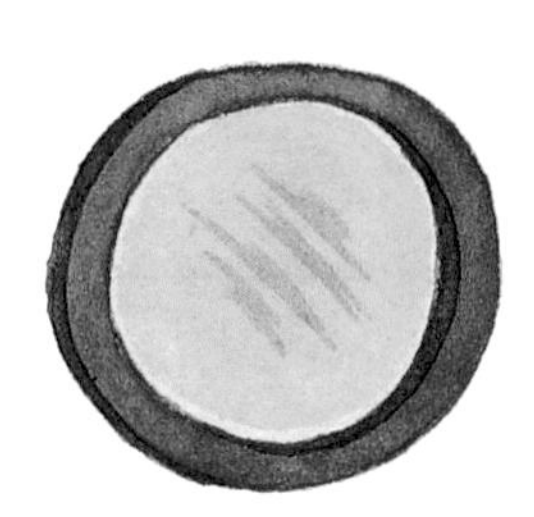

mirror
el espejo
el espeh-ho

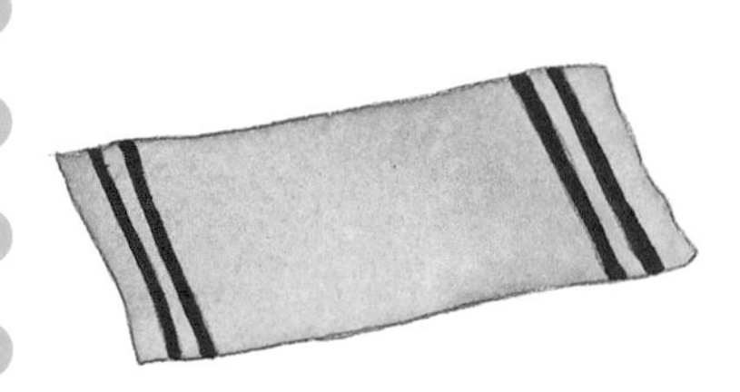

towel
la toalla
lah toh-walya

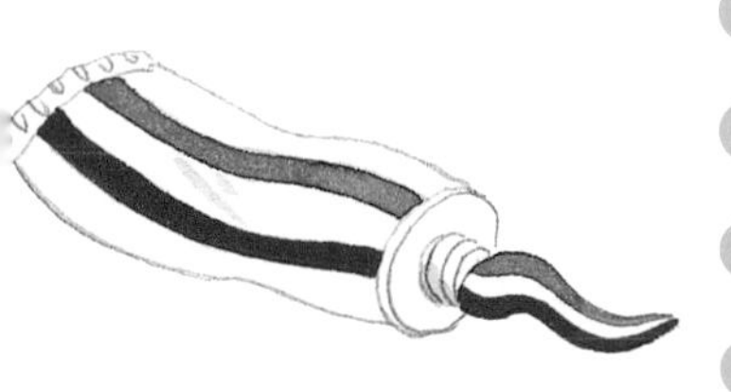

toothpaste
la pasta de dientes
lah pasta deh dee-yentes

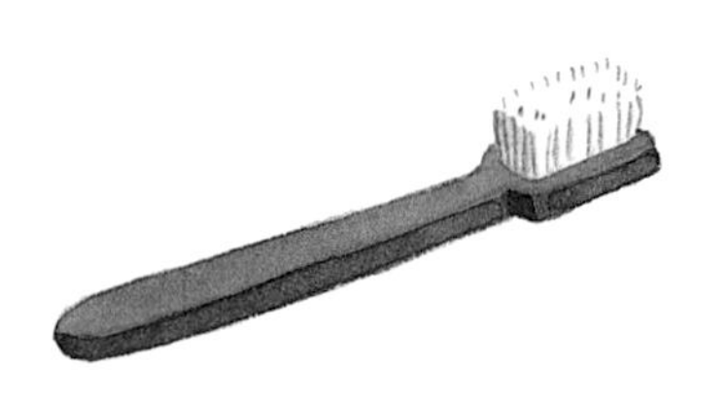

toothbrush
el cepillo de dientes
el thepee-yo deh deeyentes

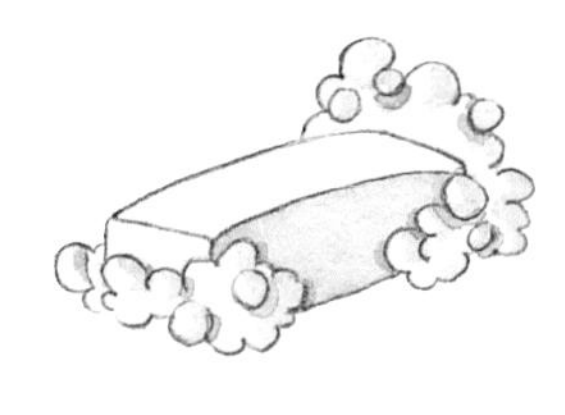

soap
el jabón
el habbon

The town – La ciudad

lah thee-oo-dad

house
la casa
lah kah-zah

school
la escuela
lah eskweh-la

station
la estación
lah es-stass-yon

shop
la tienda
la tee-enda

post office
la oficina de correos
lah ofeesee-na deh korr-eh-oss

supermarket
el supermercado
el soopair-mair-kah-do

factory
la fábrica
la fah-breeka

market
el mercado
el mair-kah-do

cinema
el cine
el see-neh

The street – La calle
lah kah-yeh

street
la calle
lah kah-yeh

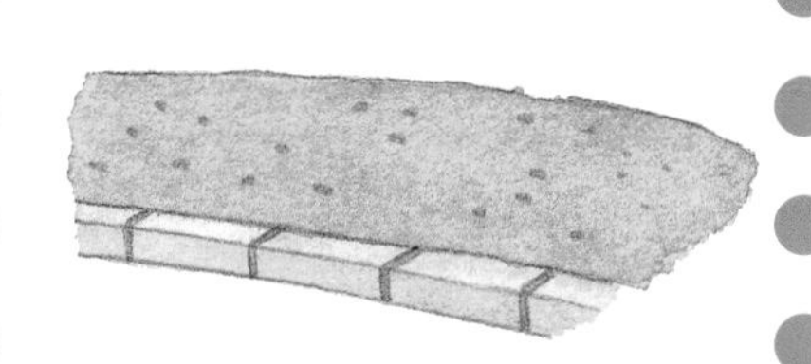

pavement
la acera
lah ah-thair-a

bus stop
la parada
lah parah-da

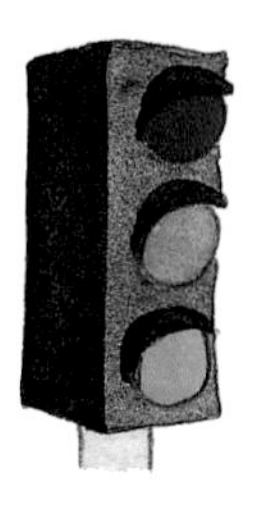

traffic lights
el semáforo
el semah-foro

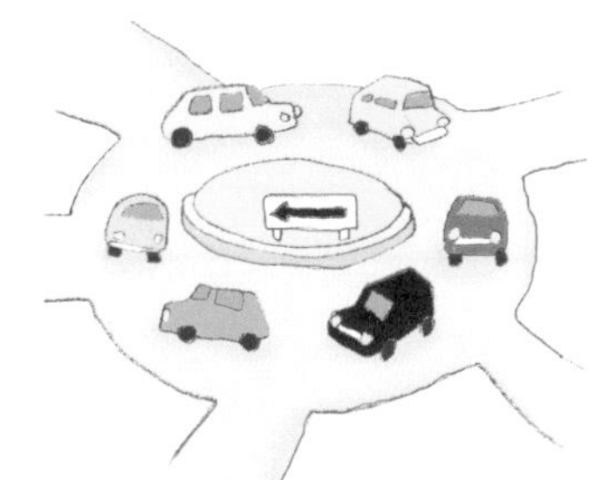

roundabout
la rotonda
lah roh-ton-da

streetlamp
la farola
lah fah-roll-a

road sign
la señal de tráfico
lah senyal deh trafeeko

zebra crossing
el paso de cebra
el pass-o deh theh-bra

police
el policía
el poleethee-ya

bus
el autobús
el aowtoboos

ambulance
la ambulancia
lah amboo-lan-theea

bicycle
la bicicleta
lah beetheekletta

car
el coche
el kocheh

police car
el coche de policía
el kocheh deh poleethee-ya

motorbike
la motocicleta
lah moto-thee-klet-a

lorry
el camión
el kam-yon

fire engine
el coche de bomberos
el kocheh deh bombair-oss

van
la furgoneta
lah foorgonay-ta

The park – El parque

el parkeh

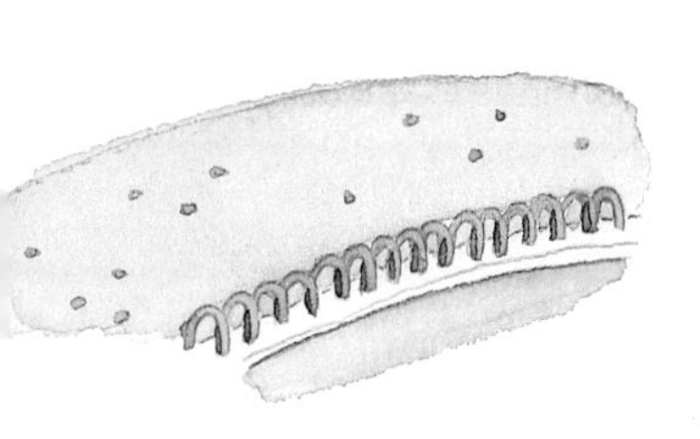

path
el camino
el kam-een-o

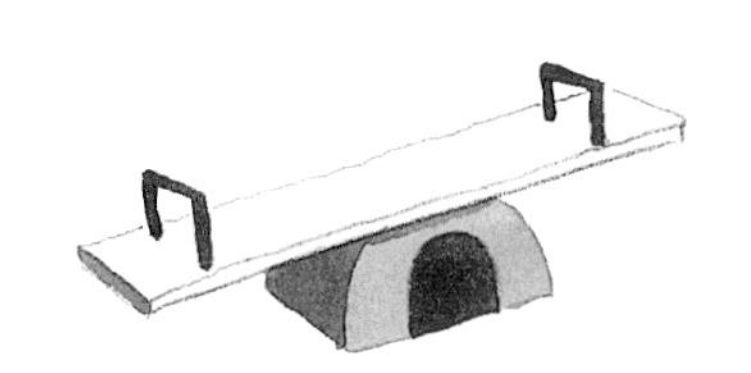

see-saw
el balancín
el balan-seen

swing
el columpio
el kol-oom-pee-o

girl
la niña
lah neen-yah

boy
el niño
el neen-yo

child
el niño/la niña
el neen-yo/la neen-ya

lake
el lago
el lah-go

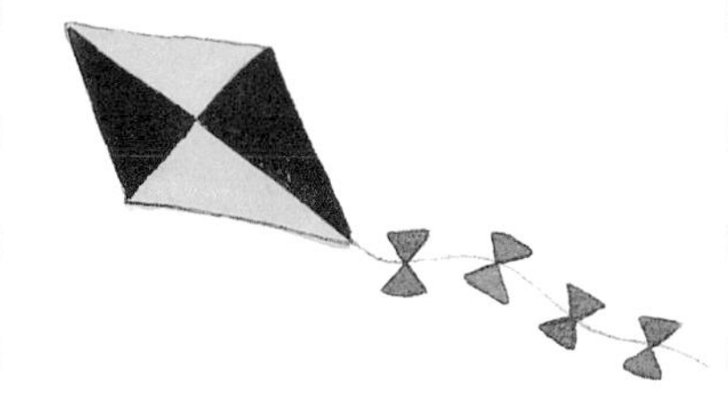

kite
la cometa
lah koh-may-ta

bench
el banco
el ban-ko

doctor
la doctora
la dok-tora

nurse
el enfermero
el enfairmairo

x-ray
la radiografía
radeeo-grafee-ah

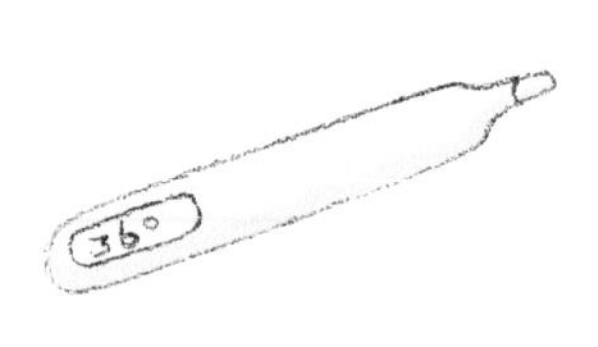

thermometer
el termómetro
el tair-momeh-tro

medicine
la medicina
lah medee-theena

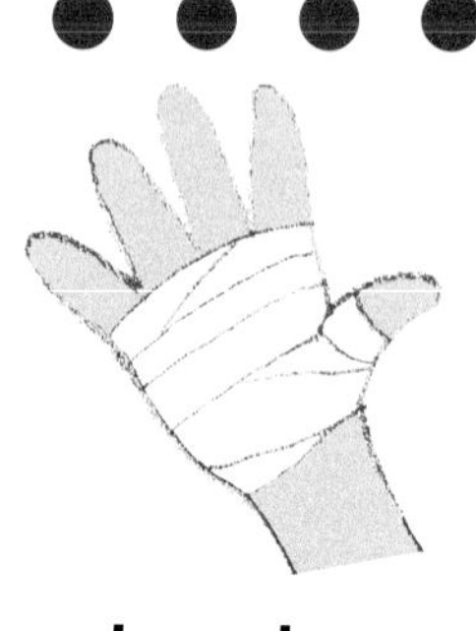

bandage
el vendaje
el benda-heh

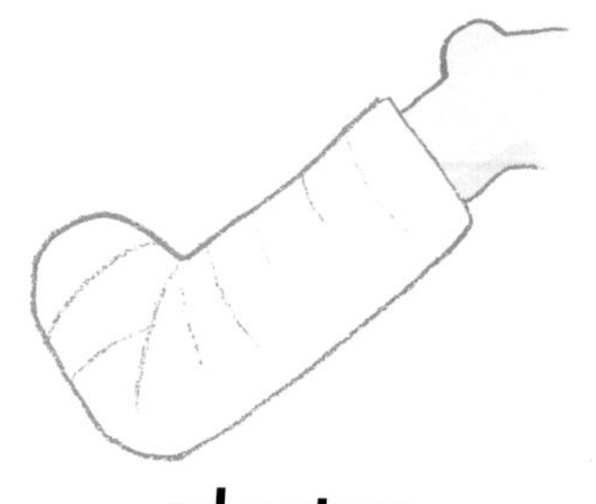

plaster
la escayola
lah eskah-yola

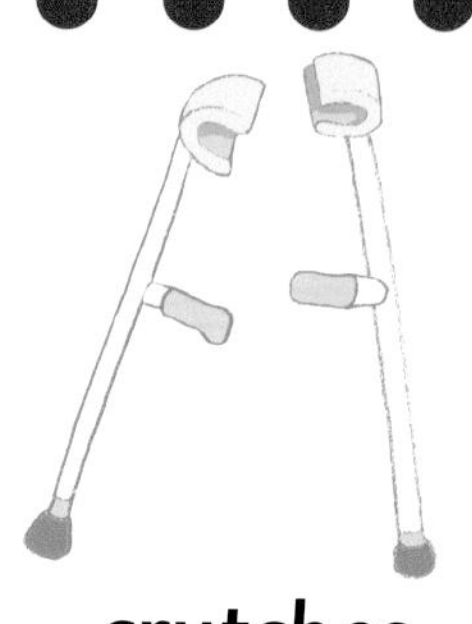

crutches
las muletas
lass mooleh-tass

wheelchair
la silla de ruedas
la seeya deh roo-eh-dass

The supermarket – El supermercado

el soopair-mair-kah-do

egg
el huevo
el lway-bo

bread
el pan
el pan

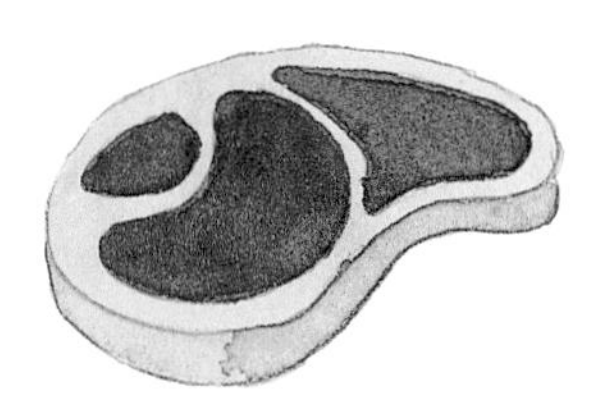

meat
la carne
lah kar-neh

rice
el arroz
el ah-roth

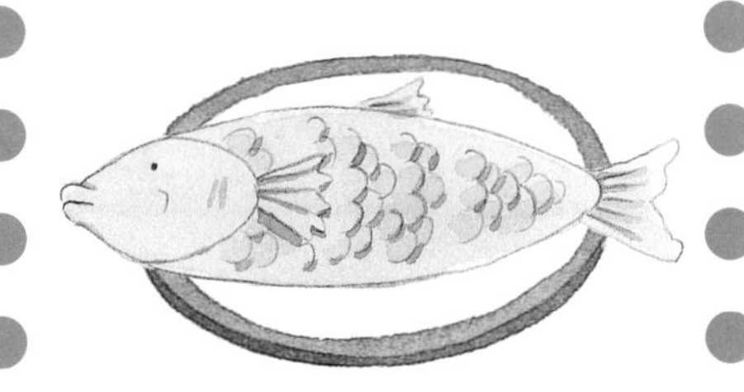

fish
el pescado
el peskah-do

butter
la mantequilla
lah manteh-kee-ya

milk
la leche
lah leh-cheh

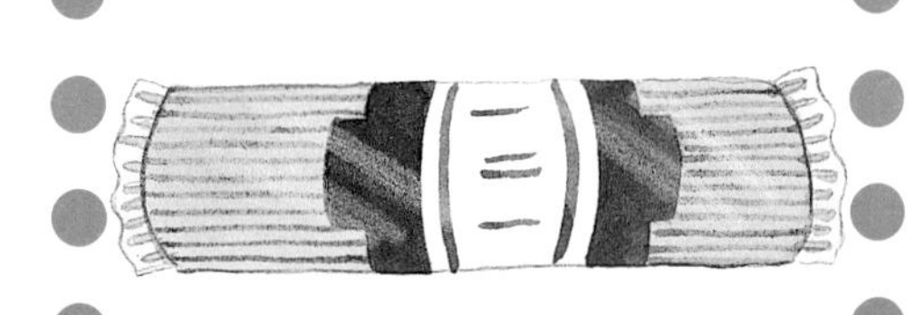

pasta
la pasta
lah pas-tah

sugar
el azúcar
el as-thoo-kar

Fruit – La fruta

lah froo-ta

apple
la manzana
lah man-thah-na

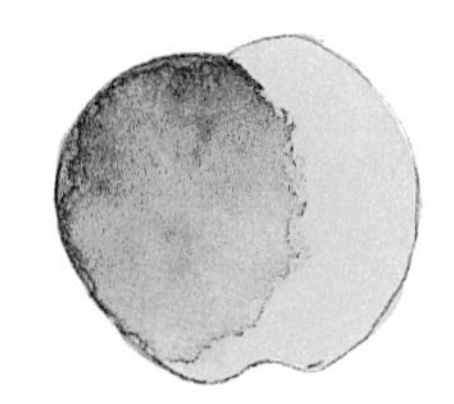

peach
el melocotón
el meh-lo-koton

cherry
la cereza
lah thair-ay-sah

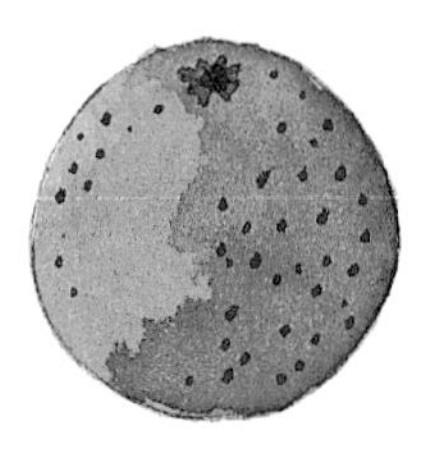

orange
la naranja
lah nah-ran-hah

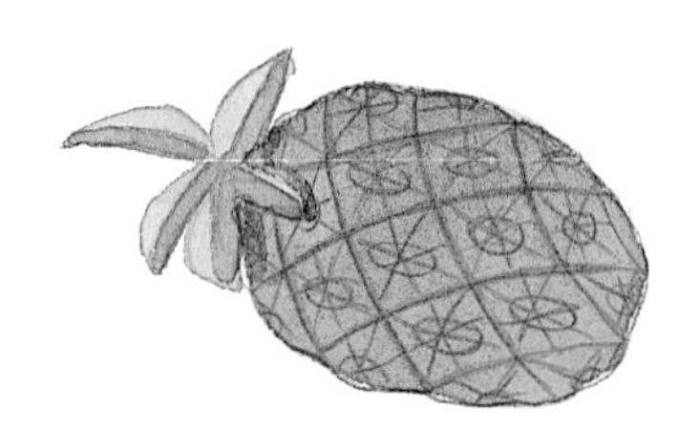

pineapple
la piña
lah peen-yah

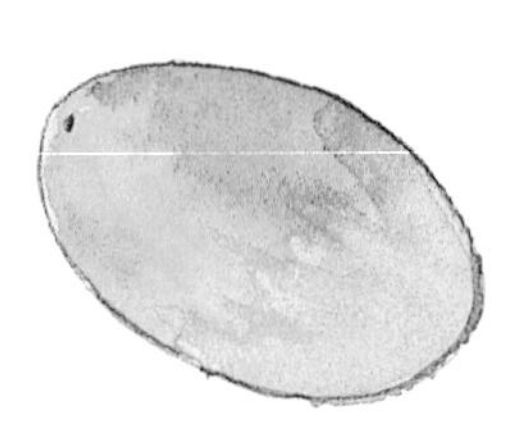

mango
el mango
el mango

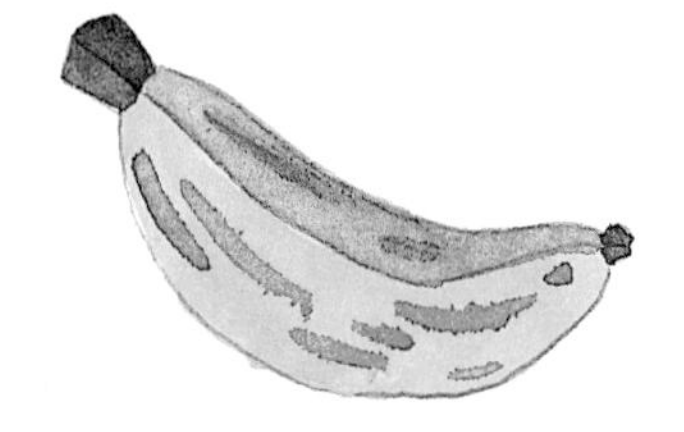

banana
el plátano
el plah-tan-o

grapes
las uvas
lass oobass

strawberry
la fresa
lah fray-sa

Vegetables – Las verduras

lass bair-<u>doo</u>-rass

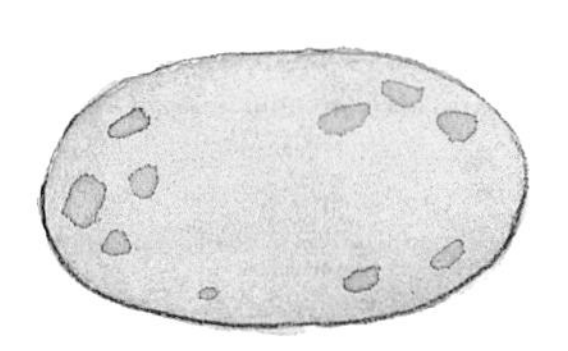

potato
la patata
la pah-<u>tah</u>-ta

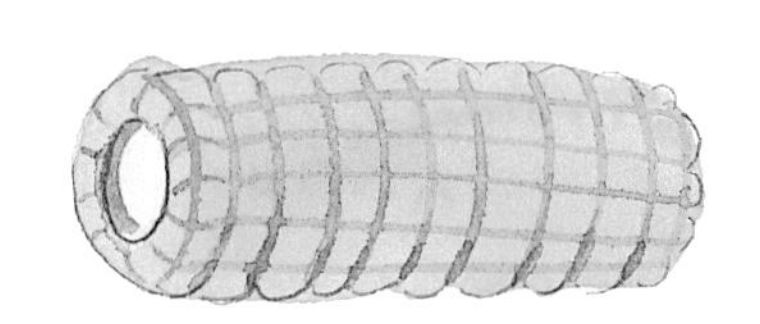

corn
el maíz
el mah-<u>eess</u>

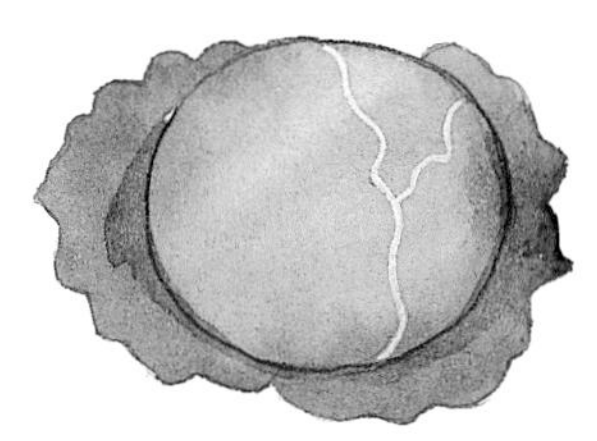

cabbage
la col
lah kol

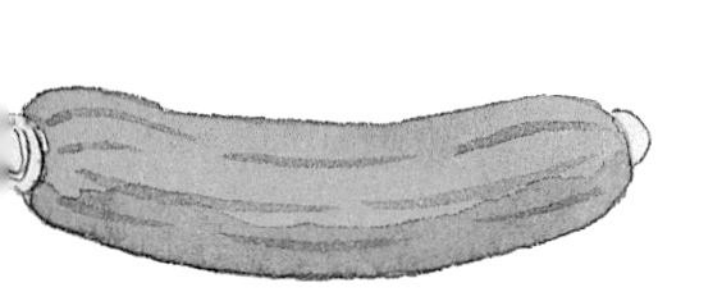

courgette
el calabacín
el kalah-bah-<u>theen</u>

carrot
la zanahoria
lah thanah-<u>or</u>-ee-a

aubergine
la berenjena
lah bairen-<u>hay</u>-na

tomato
el tomate
el tom-<u>ah</u>-teh

lettuce
la lechuga
lah let<u>choo</u>-gah

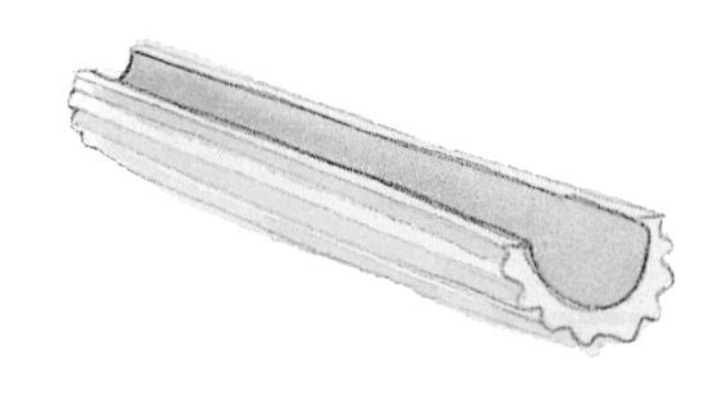

celery
el apio
el <u>ah</u>-pee-o

The country- El campo

el kampo

tree

el árbol

el ar-bol

grass

la hierba

lah yair-ba

flower

la flor

lah flor

field

el prado

el prah-do

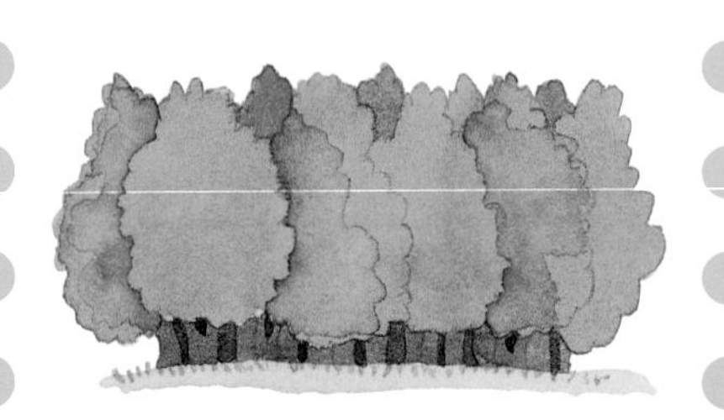

forest

el bosque

el bos-keh

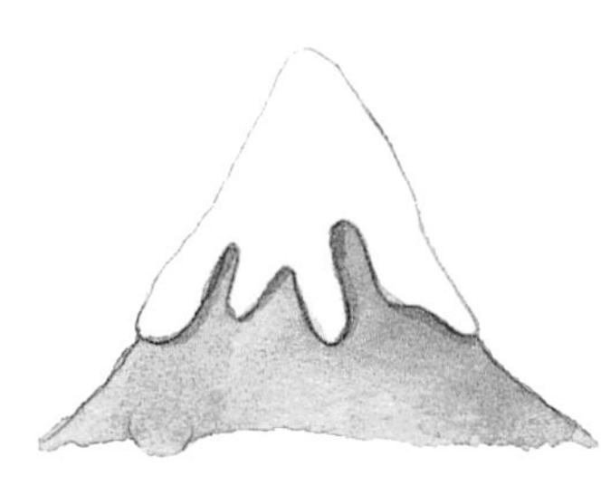

mountain

la montaña

lah mon-tan-ya

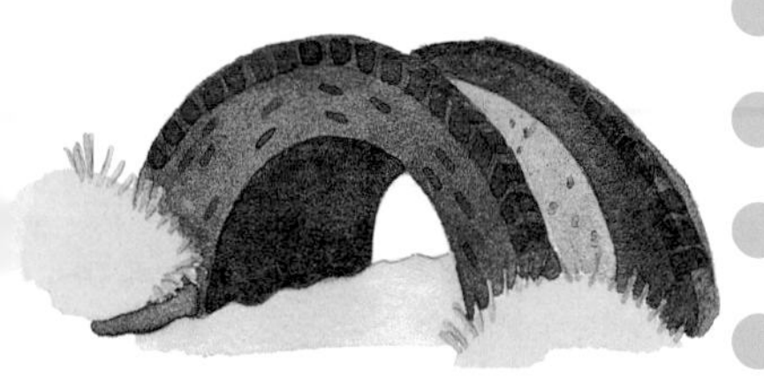

bridge

el puente

el pwen-teh

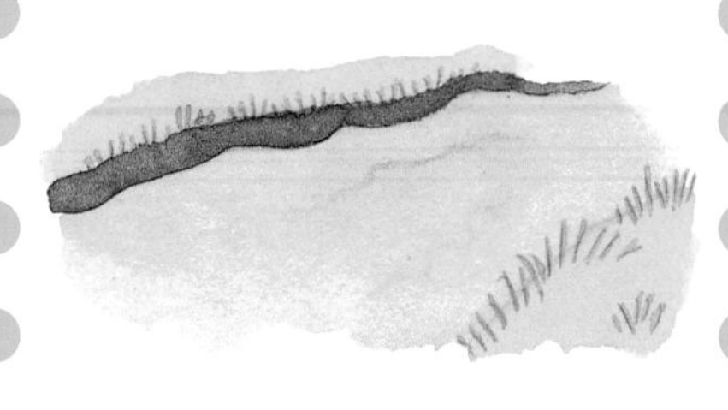

river

el río

el ree-oh

bird

el pájaro

el pa-ha-roh

In the forest – En el bosque

en el boskeh

fox
el zorro
el thor-roh

squirrel
la ardilla
lah ardee-ya

deer
el ciervo
el see-air-bo

rabbit
el conejo
el kon-ay-ho

brown bear
el oso marrón
el oh-so mar-on

butterfly
la mariposa
lah maree-poh-sa

beetle
el escarabajo
el eskah-rah-bah-ho

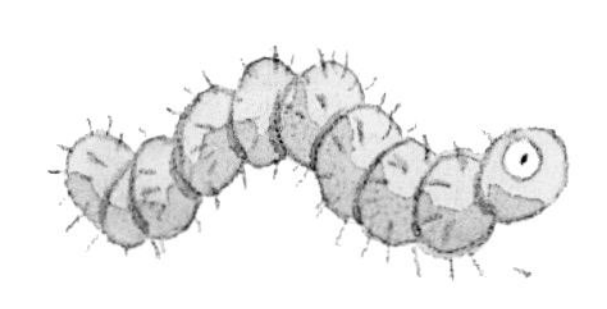

caterpillar
la oruga
la oroo-ga

fly
la mosca
lah moss-ka

The farm – La granja

lah gran-ha

cat

el gato

el gah-to

mouse

el ratón

el rah-ton

dog

el perro

el peh-ro

cow

la vaca

lah bah-ka

horse

el caballo

el kah-bal-yo

pig

el cerdo

el sair-do

sheep

la oveja

lah obeh-ha

duck

el pato

el pah-to

goat

la cabra

lah kah-bra

Baby animals – Las crías de animales

lass cree-ass deh aneemah-less

puppy
el cachorro
el kachor-o

kitten
el gatito
el gat-eet-o

foal
el potro
el pot-ro

calf
el ternero
el tair-nair-o

chick
el pollito
el poyeet-o

cygnet
el cisne pequeñito
el theesneh peken-yeet-o

duckling
el patito
el pateet-o

lamb
el cordero
el kordair-o

piglet
el cerdito
el thair-deet-o

At the beach – En la playa

en lah plah-ya

sea
el mar
el mar

seagull
la gaviota
lah gab-yota

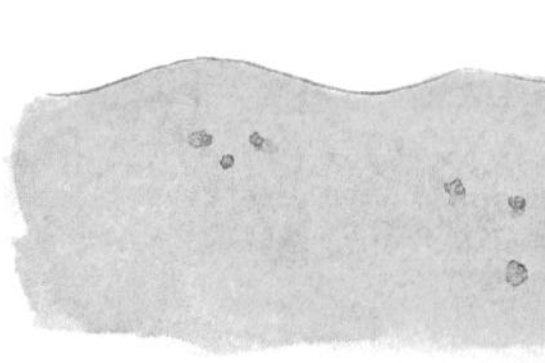

sand
la arena
lah areh-na

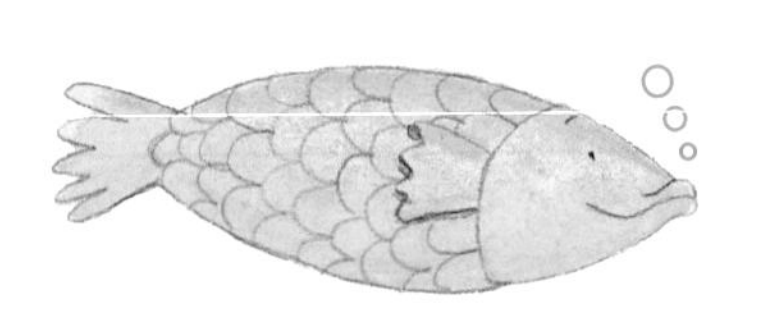

fish
el pez
el peth

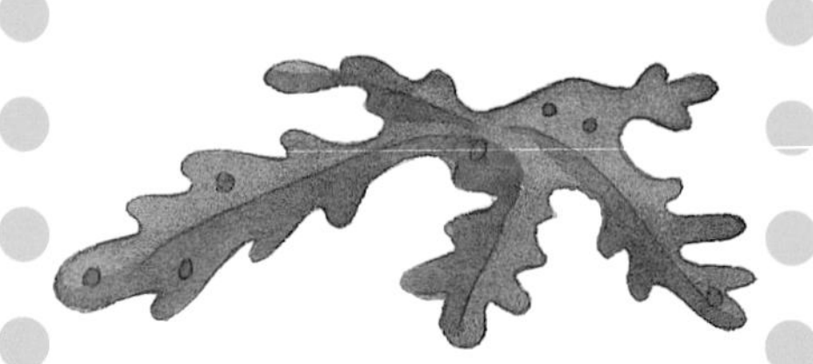

seaweed
el alga marina
el alga mareena

shell
la concha
lah koncha

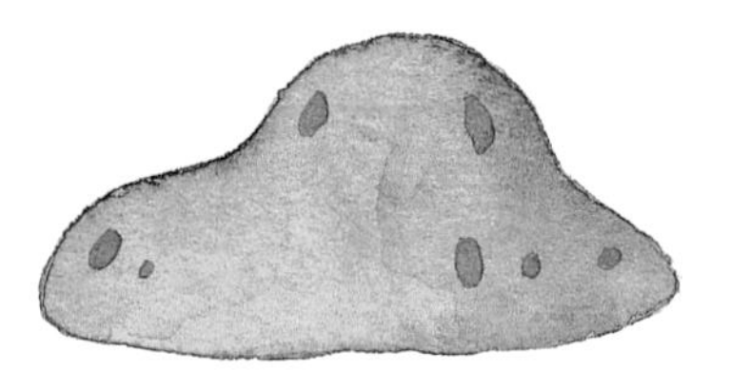

rock
la roca
lah rokka

sailing boat
el velero
el belair-o

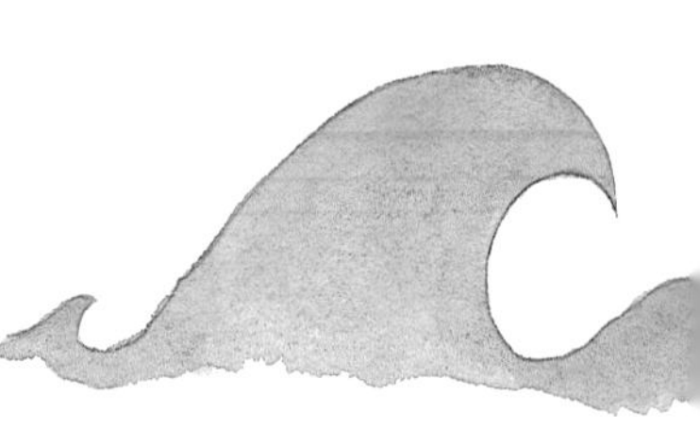

wave
la ola
lah oh-la

Under the sea – Bajo el mar

bah-ho el mar

octopus
el pulpo
el pool-po

starfish
la estrella de mar
lah estreh-ya deh mar

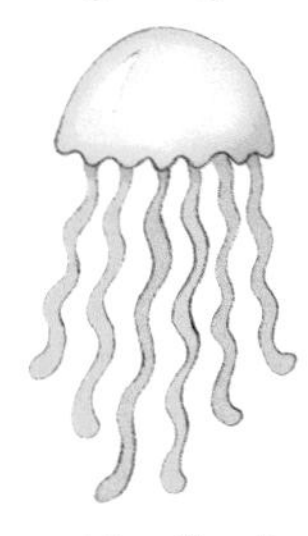

jellyfish
la medusa
lah medoo-za

lobster
la langosta
lah langoo-sta

shark
el tiburón
el teeboo-ron

whale
la ballena
lah bal-eh-na

wreck
el naufragio
el now-frah-hee-o

diver
el buceador
el boo-theh-ah-dor

coral
el coral
el koral

The zoo – El zoo

el thoo

giraffe
la jirafa
lah hee-rah-fa

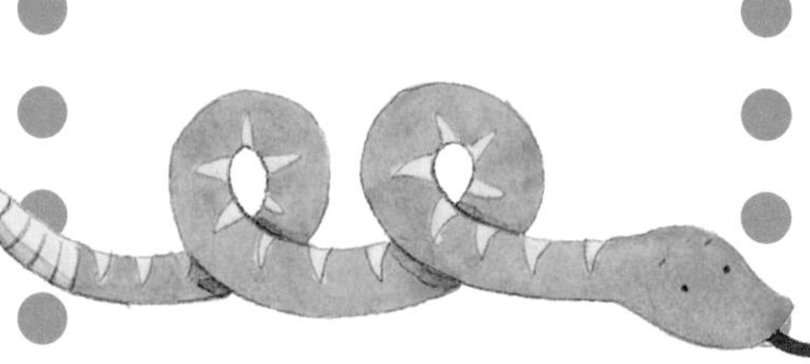

snake
la serpiente
lah sairp-yen-teh

hippopotamus
el hipopótamo
el eepo-pot-tam-o

dolphin
el delfín
el del-feen

tiger
el tigre
el tee-greh

crocodile
el cocodrilo
el kokko-dree-lo

polar bear
el oso polar
el osso pol-lar

lion
el león
el leh-on

elephant
el elefante
el eleh-fan-teh

Toys – Los juguetes

loss hoo<u>gait</u>-ess

teddy
el osito
el o-<u>seet</u>-o

robot
el robot
el roh-<u>bot</u>

ball
la pelota
lah peh-<u>loh</u>-ta

puzzle
el rompecabezas
el rompeh-kah-<u>beth</u>ass

toy train
el trenecito de juguete
el treneh-<u>thee</u>to deh hoo<u>gait</u>-eh

game
el juego
el <u>hweh</u>-go

doll
la muñeca
lah moon-<u>yeh</u>-ka

paints
las pinturas
lass peen-<u>too</u>-rass

drum
el tambor
el tam<u>bor</u>

Party time! – ¡Fiesta!

fee-essta

sandwich
el bocadillo
el bokadee-yo

chocolate
el chocolate
el chokko-lah-teh

chips
las patatas fritas
las pah-tah-tass free-tas

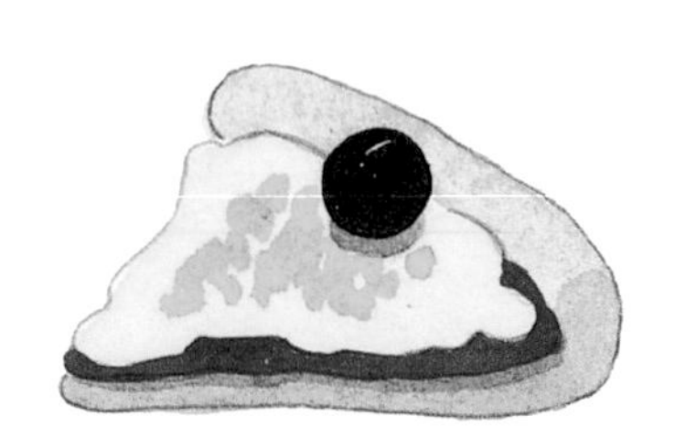

pizza
la pizza
lah peet-za

cake
el pastel
el pas-tel

ice-cream
el helado
el el-lah-doh

cola
el refresco
el reh-fresk-o

orange juice
el zumo de naranja
el thoo-moh deh nar-ran-ha

water
el agua
el ag-wa

The classroom – La clase

lah klass-eh

teacher
la profesora
lah professor-ra

table
la mesa
lah messa

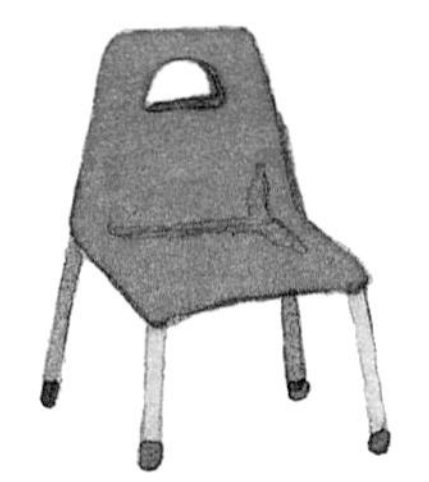

chair
la silla
lah see-ya

book
el libro
el leebro

coloured pencil
el lápiz de color
el lah-peeth deh kolor

glue
el pegamento
el peg-amento

paper
el papel
el pap-el

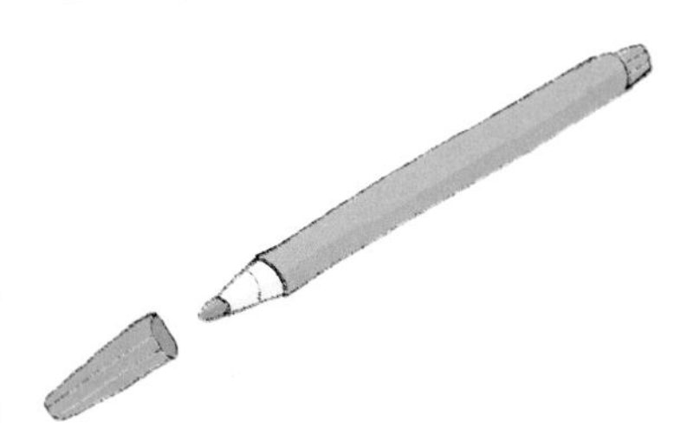

pen
la pluma
lah plooma

scissors
las tijeras
lass tee-hair-ass

football
el fútbol
el foot-bol

table tennis
el ping pong
el peeng-pong

skiing
esquiar
ess-kee-ar

gymnastics
la gimnasia
lah gym-nah-zeeah

cycling
ir en bicicleta
eer en bee-thee-klet-a

athletics
el atletismo
el atlet-eezmo

fishing
pescar
pess-kar

swimming
nadar
nah-dar

basketball
el baloncesto
el balon-thess-sto

Weather – El tiempo

el tee-empo

sun
el sol
el sol

hot
calor
kah-lor

rain
llueve
lwaybeh

cloud
la nube
lah noo-beh

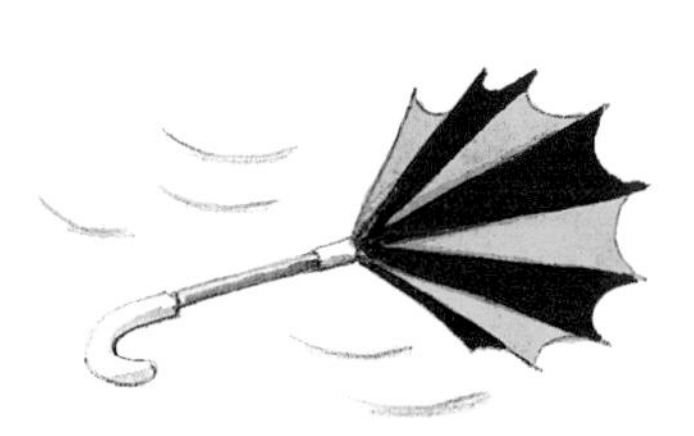

wind
el viento
el bee-en-toh

storm
la tormenta
la tormen-tah

fog
la niebla
la nee-aybla

cold
frío
free-o

snow
nieva
nee-ay-bah

Action words – *Palabras de acción*

pah-<u>lab</u>-rass deh athee-<u>on</u>

running
correr
koh-<u>rair</u>

walking
andar
an<u>dar</u>

crawling
gatear
gateh-<u>ar</u>

carrying
cargar
kar<u>gar</u>

standing
estar de pie
es<u>tar</u> deh pee-<u>eh</u>

sitting
estar sentado
es<u>tar</u> sen<u>tah</u>-do

pushing
empujar
empoo-<u>har</u>

hugging
abrazar
abra<u>thar</u>

pulling
estirar
ess-tee<u>rar</u>

Storybooks – Los libros de cuentos

loss leebross deh koo-en-toss

dragon
el dragón
el drah-gon

mermaid
la sirena
lah see-rain-a

knight
el caballero
el kaba-yair-o

pirate
el pirata
el pee-rah-ta

fairy
el hada
el ah-da

witch
la bruja
lah broo-ha

prince
el príncipe
el preen-thee-peh

princess
la princesa
lah preen-thessa

castle
el castillo
el kastee-yo

The building site – La obra

lah ob-ra

digger
la excavadora
lah eskaba-dor-a

cement mixer
el camión hormigonera
el kam-yon ormee-gon-aira

crane
la grúa
lah groo-a

scaffolding
el andamio
el andah-mee-o

dumper truck
el camión volquete
el kam-yon bolket-eh

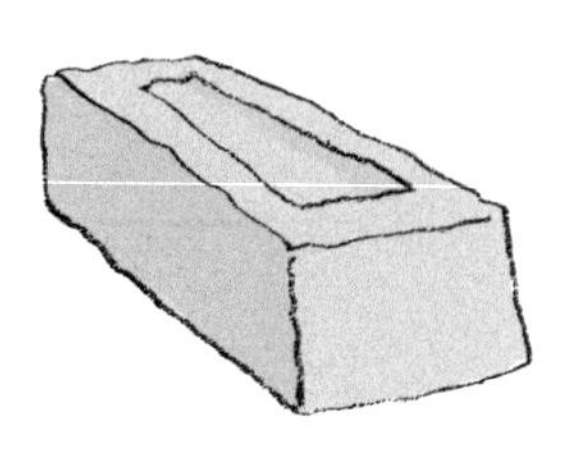

brick
el ladrillo
el ladree-yo

bulldozer
el bulldozer
el bool-doth-air

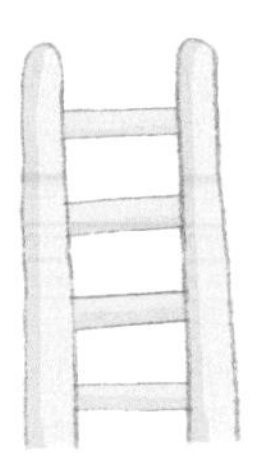

ladder
la escalera
lah eskalair-a

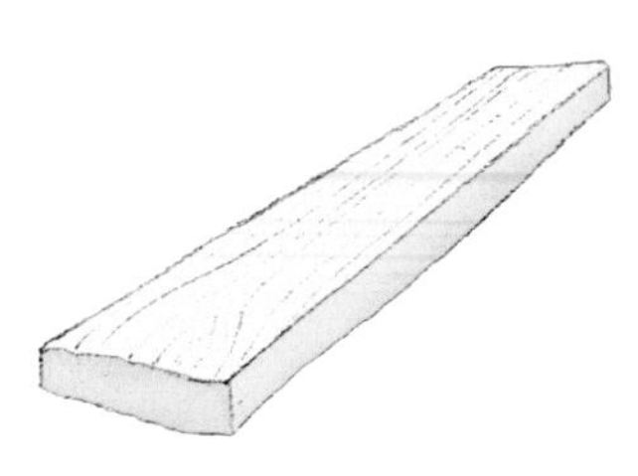

wood
el tablón
el tab-lon

Tools – Las herramientas

lass aira-mee-entass

rake
el rastrillo
el rastree-yo

spade
la pala
la pah-la

bucket
el cubo
el koo-bo

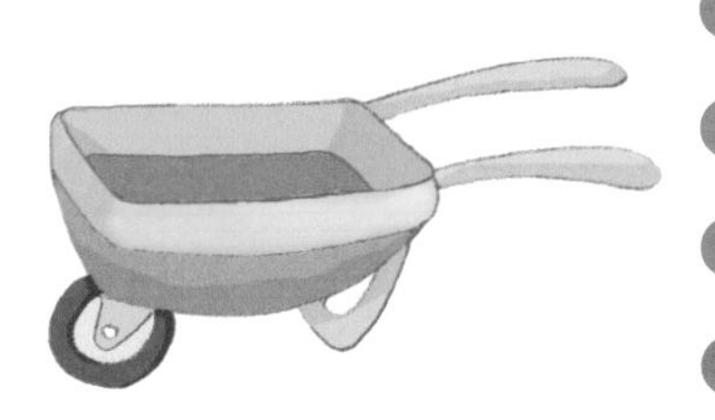

wheelbarrow
la carretilla
lah karetee-ya

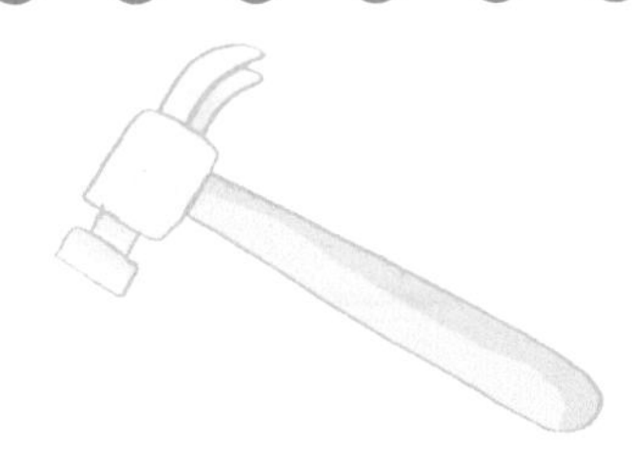

hammer
el martillo
el mahtee-yo

nail
el clavo
el klah-bo

saw
el serrucho
el sair-oocho

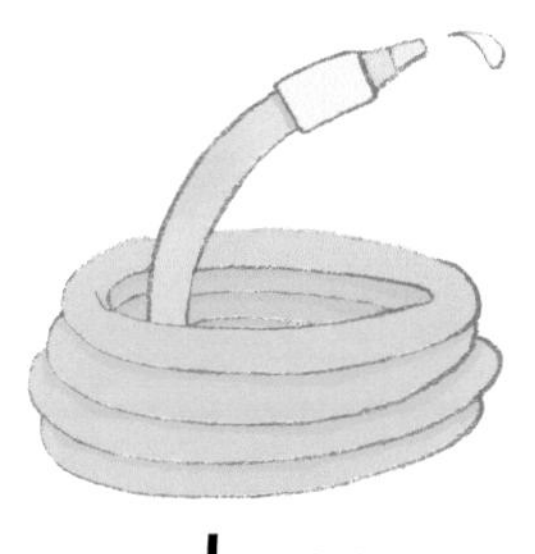

hose
la manguera
lah man-gair-a

paintbrush
la brocha
lah brocha

Luggage – El equipaje

el ekeepa-heh

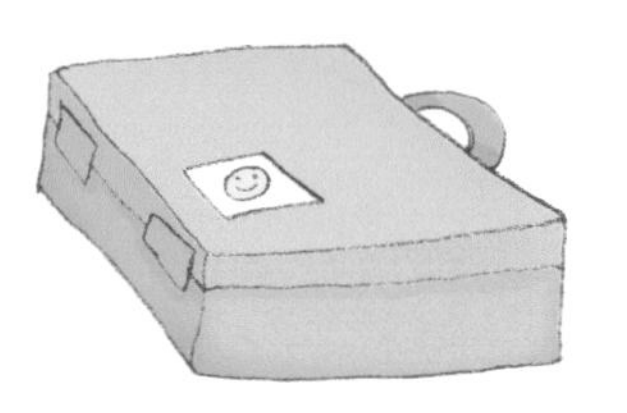

suitcase
la maleta
lah maleh-ta

satchel
el morral
el mor-al

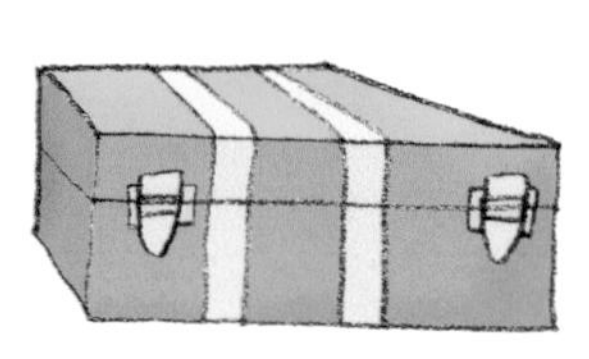

trunk
el baúl
el bah-ool

rucksack
la mochila
lah mochee-la

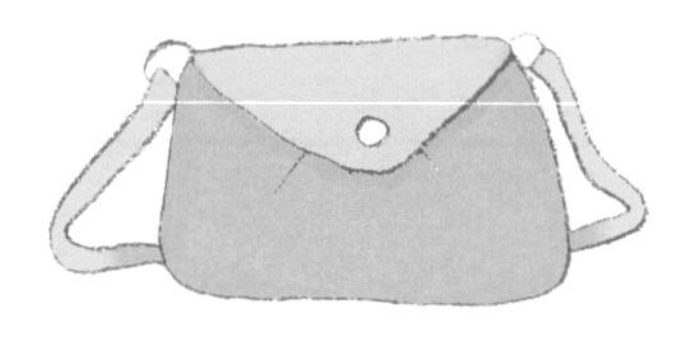

handbag
el bolso de señora
el bolso deh senyor-a

briefcase
el maletín
el malet-een

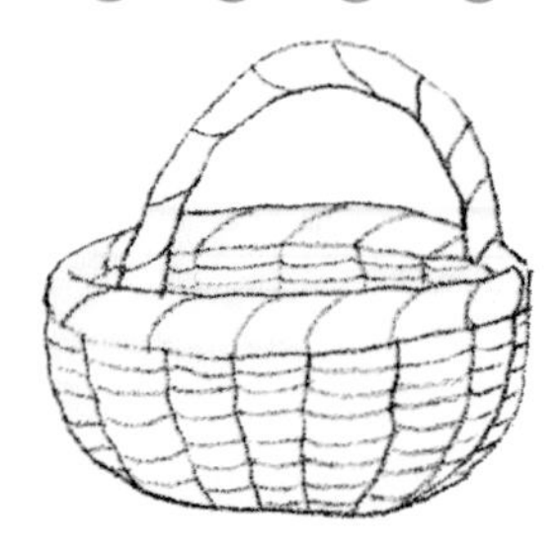

basket
la cesta
lah thess-ta

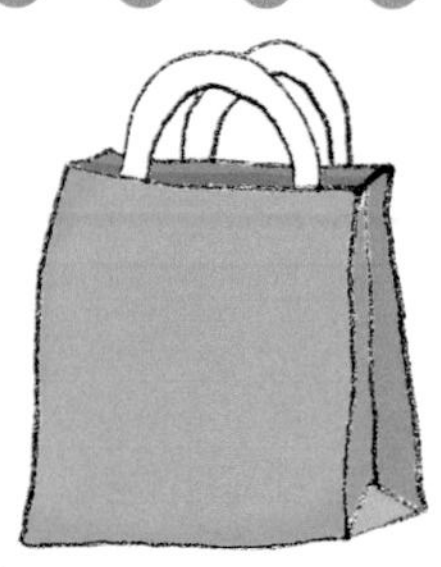

shopping bag
la bolsa de la compra
lah bolsa deh lah kompra

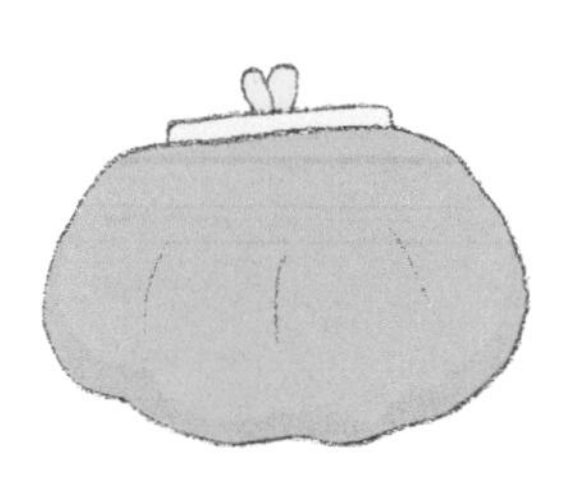

purse
el monedero
el moned-air-o

Rail travel – El viaje en tren

el bee-ah-heh en tren

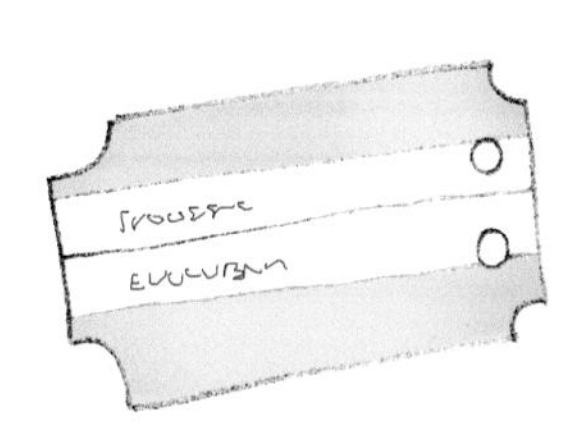

ticket
el billete
el bee-yet-eh

ticket collector
el revisor
el reb-ee-sor

platform
el andén
el anden

train driver
la maquinista
lah makeen-eesta

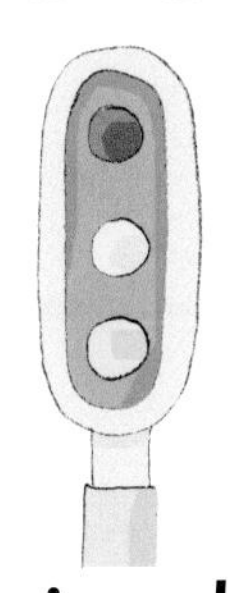

signal
la señal
lah senyal

train
el tren
el tren

seat
el asiento
el assee-ento

level crossing
el paso a nivel
el pah-so ah neebel

rails
los raíles
los rah-ee-less

Air travel – El viaje en avión

el bee-ah-heh en abee-on

aeroplane
el avión
el abee-on

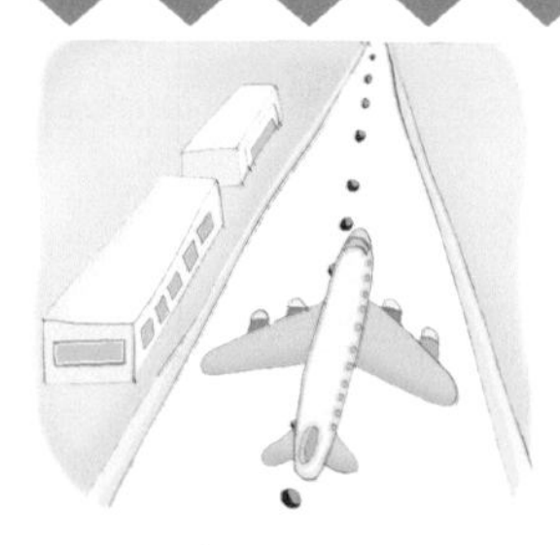

airport
el aeropuerto
el ah-airo-poo-airto

pilot
el piloto
el pee-lot-o

flight attendant
la azafata
lah atha-fat-a

x-ray machine
el detector de rayos x
el detek-tor deh rah-yoss eeks

passport
el pasaporte
el passa-port-eh

trolley
el carrito
el kareeto

snack
el aperitivo
el apairee-teebo

seatbelt
el cinturón de segurida
el theen-too-ron deh segooree-d

At sea – En el mar

en el mar

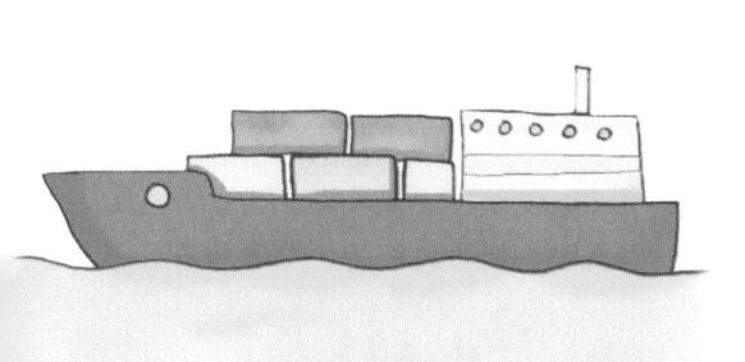

ship
el barco
el barko

yacht
el yate
el yat-eh

rowing boat
el bote a remos
el boteh ah reh-moss

tanker
el petrolero
el petrol-airo

fishing boat
el barco de pesca
el barko deh peska

ferry
el ferry
el fairee

buoy
la boya
lah boy-a

port
el puerto
el poo-airto

lighthouse
el faro
el fah-ro

Opposites – Los contrarios

loss kon-trah-reeoss

friendly

amable

amah-bleh

angry

enfadado/enfadada

enfath-ah-do/enfath-ah-da

thin

delgado/delgada

del-gah-do/del-gah-da

clean

limpio/limpia

leem-pee-o/leem-pee-a

dirty

sucio/sucia

soothee-o/soothee-a

tidy

ordenado/ordenada

ordenah-do/ordenah-da

sad

triste

treess-teh

happy

feliz

fel-eeth

heavy

pesado/pesada

pezah-do/pezah-da

Opposites – Los contrarios

loss kon-trah-reeoss

fat
gordo/gorda
gor-do/gor-da

tall
alto/alta
alto/alta

short
bajo/baja
bah-ho/bah-ha

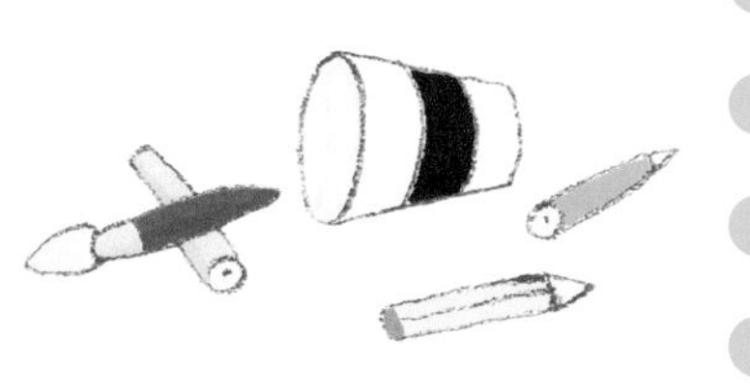

messy
esordenado/desordenada
z-ordenah-do/dez-ordenah-da

fast
rápido/rápida
rah-peedo/rah-peeda

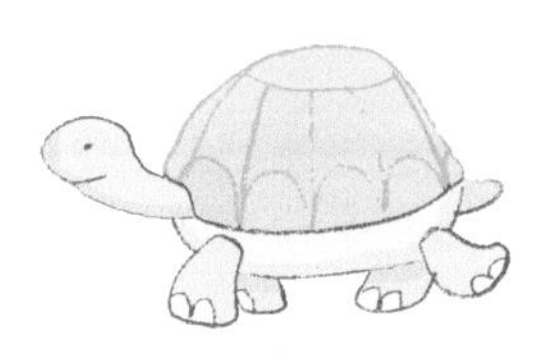

slow
lento/lenta
lento/lenta

light
ligero/ligera
lee-jairo/lee-jaira

beautiful
hermoso/hermosa
airmo-so/airmo-sa

ugly
feo/fea
feh-o/feh-a

Spanish/español – English/inglés

abrazar to hug
el abrigo coat
la abuela grandmother
el abuelo grandfather
la acera pavement
el aeropuerto airport
el agua water
la alfombra rug
el alga marina seaweed
alto/alta tall
amable friendly
amarillo/amarilla yellow
la ambulancia ambulance
el andamio scaffolding
andar to walk
el andén platform
el aperitivo snack
el apio celery
el árbol tree
la ardilla squirrel
la arena sand
el armario wardrobe
el arroz rice
el asiento seat
el atletismo athletics
el autobús bus
el avión aeroplane
la azafata flight attendant
el azúcar sugar
azul blue
bajo/baja short
el balancín see-saw
la ballena whale
el baloncesto basketball
el banco bench
la bañera bath
el barco ship
el barco de pesca fishing boat
el baúl trunk
la berenjena aubergine
la bicicleta bicycle
el billete ticket
blanco/blanca white
la boca mouth
el bocadillo sandwich
la bolsa de la compra shopping bag
el bolso de señora handbag
el bosque forest
el bote a remos rowing boat
la boya buoy
el brazo arm
la brocha paintbrush
la bruja witch
el buceador diver
el bulldozer bulldozer
el caballero knight
el caballo horse
la cabeza head
la cabra goat
la cacerola saucepan
el cachorro puppy
el calabacín courgette
los calcetines socks
la calle street
calor hot
la cama bed
el camino path
el camión lorry
el camión hormigonera cement mixer
el camión volquete dumper truck
la camisa shirt
el campo country
cargar to carry
la carne meat
la carretilla wheelbarrow
el carrito trolley
la casa house
el castillo castle
catorce fourteen
el cepillo de dientes toothbrush
el cepillo del pelo hairbrush
el cerdito piglet
el cerdo pig
la cereza cherry
la cesta basket
el chocolate chocolate
el ciervo deer
cinco five
el cine cinema
el cinturón de seguridad seatbelt
el cisne pequeñito cygnet
la ciudad town
la clase classroom
el clavo nail
el coche car
el coche de bomberos fire engine
el coche de policía police car
la cocina kitchen
la cocina cooker
el cocodrilo crocodile
el cojín cushion
la col cabbage
los colores colours
la cometa kite
la cómoda chest of drawers
la concha shell
el conejo rabbit
el coral coral
el cordero lamb
correr to run
las cortinas curtains
el cuadro picture
el cuarto de baño bathroom
cuatro four
el cubo bucket
la cuchara spoon
el cuchillo knife
el cuerpo body
el delfín dolphin
delgado/delgada thin
los deportes sports
desordenado/desordenada messy

el despertador alarm clock
el detector de rayos x x-ray machine
diecinueve nineteen
dieciocho eighteen
dieciséis sixteen
diecisiete seventeen
diez ten
doce twelve
la doctora doctor
dos two
el dragón dragon
la ducha shower
el elefante elephant
empujar to push
enfadado/enfadada angry
el enfermero nurse
el equipaje luggage
la escalera ladder
las escaleras stairs
el escarabajo beetle
la escayola plaster
la escuela school
el espejo mirror
esquiar to ski
la estación station
el estante shelf
estar de pie to be standing
estar sentado to be sitting
estirar to pull
la estrella de mar starfish
la excavadora digger
la fábrica factory
la falda skirt
la familia family
el faro lighthouse
la farola streetlamp
feliz happy
feo/fea ugly
el ferry ferry
la fiesta party
la flor flower
el fregadero sink
la fresa strawberry
el frigorífico fridge
frío cold
la fruta fruit
la furgoneta van
el fútbol football
gatear to crawl
el gatito kitten
el gato cat
la gaviota seagull
la gimnasia gymnastics
gordo/gorda fat
la granja farm
la grúa crane
la habitación bedroom
el hada fairy
el helado ice-cream
la hermana sister
el hermano brother
hermoso/hermosa beautiful
las herramientas tools
la hierba grass
el hipopótamo hippopotamus
los hombros shoulders
el hospital hospital
el huevo egg
ir en bicicleta to cycle
el jabón soap
el jardín garden
la jirafa giraffe
el juguete toy
el ladrillo brick
el lago lake
la langosta lobster
el lápiz de color coloured pencil
el lavabo washbasin
la leche milk
la lechuga lettuce
lento/lenta slow
el león lion
el libro book
ligero/ligera light
limpio/limpia clean
llueve rain
la madre mother
el maíz corn
la maleta suitcase
el maletín briefcase
mamá Mummy
el mango mango
la manguera hose
la mano hand
la mantequilla butter
la manzana apple
la maquinista train driver
el mar sea
la mariposa butterfly
marrón brown
el martillo hammer
la medicina medicine
la medusa jellyfish
el melocotón peach
el mercado market
la mesa table
la mochila rucksack
el monedero purse
la montaña mountain
morado/morada purple
el morral satchel
la mosca fly
la motocicleta motorbike
las muletas crutches
la muñeca doll
nadar to swim
la naranja orange (fruit)
naranja orange (colour)
la nariz nose
el naufragio wreck
negro/negra black
la niebla fog
nieva snow
la niña girl
el niño boy
el niño/la niña child
la nube cloud
nueve nine
la obra building site
ocho eight
la oficina de correos post office
los ojos eyes
la ola wave
once eleven
ordenado/ordenada tidy

el ordenador computer
la oruga caterpillar
el osito teddy
el oso marrón brown bear
el oso polar polar bear
la oveja sheep
el padre father
el pájaro bird
la pala spade
el pan bread
el pantalón trousers
papá Daddy
el papel paper
la parada bus stop
el pasaporte passport
el paso a nivel level crossing
el paso de cebra zebra crossing
la pasta pasta
la pasta de dientes toothpaste
el pastel cake
la patata potato
las patatas fritas chips
el patito duckling
el pato duck
el pegamento glue
la pelota ball
el perro dog
pesado/pesada heavy
el pescado fish (to eat)
pescar to fish
el petrolero tanker
el pez fish (in the sea)
el pie foot
la pierna leg
el pijama pyjamas
el piloto pilot
la piña pineapple
el ping pong table tennis
las pinturas paints
el pirata pirate
la pizza pizza
el plátano banana
el plato plate
la playa beach
la pluma pen
el policía police
el pollito chick
el potro foal
el prado field
los primos cousins
la princesa princess
el príncipe prince
la profesora teacher
el puente bridge
la puerta door
el puerto port
el pulpo octopus
quince fifteen
la radiografía x-ray
los raíles rails
rápido/rápida fast
el rastrillo rake
el ratón mouse
el refresco cola
el revisor ticket collector
el río river
el robot robot
la roca rock
rojo/roja red
el rompecabezas puzzle
la ropa clothes
la rotonda roundabout
el salón sitting room
seis six
el semáforo traffic lights
la señal signal
la señal de tráfico road sign
la serpiente snake
el serrucho saw
siete seven
la silla chair
la silla de ruedas wheelchair
el sillón armchair
la sirena mermaid
el sofá sofa
el sol sun
el sombrero hat
sucio/sucia dirty
el suelo floor
el supermercado supermarket
el tablón wood
el taburete stool
el tambor drum
el techo ceiling
el teléfono telephone
la televisión television
el tenedor fork
el termómetro thermometer
el ternero calf
la tía aunt
el tiburón shark
el tiempo weather
la tienda shop
el tigre tiger
las tijeras scissors
el tío uncle
la toalla towel
el tomate tomato
la tormenta storm
trece thirteen
el tren train
el trenecito de juguete toy train
tres three
triste sad
uno/una one
las uvas grapes
la vaca cow
el vaso glass
el váter toilet
los vehículos vehicles
veinte twenty
el velero sailing boat
el vendaje bandage
la ventana window
verde green
las verduras vegetables
el vestido dress
el viaje travel
el viento wind
el yate yacht
la zanahoria carrot
los zapatos shoes
el zoo zoo
el zorro fox
el zumo de naranja orange juice

English/inglés – Spanish/español

aeroplane el avión
airport el aeropuerto
alarm clock el despertador
ambulance la ambulancia
angry enfadado/enfadada
apple la manzana
arm el brazo
armchair el sillón
athletics el atletismo
aubergine la berenjena
aunt la tía
ball la pelota
banana el plátano
bandage el vendaje
basket la cesta
basketball el baloncesto
bath la bañera
bathroom el cuarto de baño
beach la playa
beautiful hermoso/hermosa
bed la cama
bedroom la habitación
beetle el escarabajo
bench el banco
bicycle la bicicleta
bird el pájaro
black negro/negra
blue azul
body el cuerpo
book el libro
boy el niño
bread el pan
brick el ladrillo
bridge el puente
briefcase el maletín
brother el hermano
brown marrón
brown bear el oso marrón
bucket el cubo
building site la obra
bulldozer el bulldozer
buoy la boya
bus el autobús
bus stop la parada
butter la mantequilla
butterfly la mariposa
cabbage la col
cake el pastel
calf el ternero
car el coche
carrot la zanahoria
to carry cargar
castle el castillo
cat el gato
caterpillar la oruga
ceiling el techo
celery el apio
cement mixer el camión hormigonera
chair la silla
cherry la cereza
chest of drawers la cómoda
chick el pollito
child el niño/la niña
chips las patatas fritas
chocolate el chocolate
cinema el cine
classroom la clase
clean limpio/limpia
clothes la ropa
cloud la nube
coat el abrigo
cola el refresco
cold frío
coloured pencil el lápiz de color
colours los colores
computer el ordenador
cooker la cocina
coral el coral
corn el maíz
country el campo
courgette el calabacín
cousins los primos
cow la vaca
crane la grúa
to crawl gatear
crocodile el cocodrilo
crutches las muletas
curtains las cortinas
cushion el cojín
to cycle ir en bicicleta
cygnet el cisne pequeñito
Daddy papá
deer el ciervo
digger la excavadora
dirty sucio/sucia
diver el buceador
doctor la doctora
dog el perro
doll la muñeca
dolphin el delfín
door la puerta
dragon el dragón
dress el vestido
drum el tambor
duck el pato
duckling el patito
dumper truck el camión volquete
egg el huevo
eight ocho
eighteen dieciocho
elephant el elefante
eleven once
eyes los ojos
factory la fábrica
fairy el hada
family la familia
farm la granja
fast rápido/rápida
fat gordo/gorda
father el padre
ferry el ferry
field el prado
fifteen quince
fire engine el coche de bomberos
fish (to eat) el pescado

fish (in the sea) el pez
to fish pescar
fishing boat el barco de pesca
five cinco
flight attendant la azafata
floor el suelo
flower la flor
fly la mosca
foal el potro
fog la niebla
foot el pie
football el fútbol
forest el bosque
fork el tenedor
four cuatro
fourteen catorce
fox el zorro
fridge el frigorífico
friendly amable
fruit la fruta
garden el jardín
giraffe la jirafa
girl la niña
glass el vaso
glue el pegamento
goat la cabra
grandfather el abuelo
grandmother la abuela
grapes las uvas
grass la hierba
green verde
gymnastics la gimnasia
hairbrush el cepillo del pelo
hammer el martillo
hand la mano
handbag el bolso de señora
happy feliz
hat el sombrero
head la cabeza
heavy pesado/pesada
hippopotamus el hipopótamo
horse el caballo
hose la manguera
hospital el hospital
hot calor
house la casa
to hug abrazar
ice-cream el helado
jellyfish la medusa
kitchen la cocina
kite la cometa
kitten el gatito
knife el cuchillo
knight el caballero
ladder la escalera
lake el lago
lamb el cordero
leg la pierna
lettuce la lechuga
level crossing el paso a nivel
light ligero/ligera
lighthouse el faro
lion el león
lobster la langosta
lorry el camión
luggage el equipaje
mango el mango
market el mercado
meat la carne
medicine la medicina
mermaid la sirena
messy desordenado/desordenada
milk la leche
mirror el espejo
mother la madre
motorbike la motocicleta
mountain la montaña
mouse el ratón
mouth la boca
Mummy mamá
nail el clavo
nine nueve
nineteen diecinueve
nose la nariz
nurse el enfermero
octopus el pulpo
one uno/una
orange (fruit) la naranja
orange (colour) naranja
orange juice el zumo de naranja
paintbrush la brocha
paints las pinturas
paper el papel
party la fiesta
passport el pasaporte
pasta la pasta
path el camino
pavement la acera
peach el melocotón
pen la pluma
picture el cuadro
pig el cerdo
piglet el cerdito
pilot el piloto
pineapple la piña
pirate el pirata
pizza la pizza
plaster la escayola
plate el plato
platform el andén
polar bear el oso polar
police el policía
police car el coche de policía
port el puerto
post office la oficina de correos
potato la patata
prince el príncipe
princess la princesa
to pull estirar
puppy el cachorro
purple morado/morada
purse el monedero
to push empujar
puzzle el rompecabezas
pyjamas el pijama
rabbit el conejo
rails los raíles
rain llueve
rake el rastrillo
red rojo/roja
rice el arroz
river el río
road sign la señal de tráfico
robot el robot

rock la roca
roundabout la rotonda
rowing boat el bote a remos
rucksack la mochila
rug la alfombra
to run correr
sad triste
sailing boat el velero
sand la arena
sandwich el bocadillo
satchel el morral
saucepan la cacerola
saw el serrucho
scaffolding el andamio
school la escuela
scissors las tijeras
sea el mar
seagull la gaviota
seat el asiento
seatbelt el cinturón de seguridad
seaweed el alga marina
see-saw el balancín
seven siete
seventeen diecisiete
shark el tiburón
sheep la oveja
shelf el estante
shell la concha
ship el barco
shirt la camisa
shoes los zapatos
shop la tienda
shopping bag la bolsa de la compra
short bajo/baja
shoulders los hombros
shower la ducha
signal la señal
sink el fregadero
sister la hermana
to be sitting estar sentado
sitting room el salón
six seis
sixteen dieciséis
to ski esquiar
skirt la falda
slow lento/lenta
snack el aperitivo
snake la serpiente
snow nieva
soap el jabón
socks los calcetines
sofa el sofá
spade la pala
spoon la cuchara
sports los deportes
squirrel la ardilla
stairs las escaleras
to be standing estar de pie
starfish la estrella de mar
station la estación
stool el taburete
storm la tormenta
strawberry la fresa
street la calle
streetlamp la farola
sugar el azúcar
suitcase la maleta
sun el sol
supermarket el supermercado
to swim nadar
table la mesa
table tennis el ping pong
tall alto/alta
tanker el petrolero
teacher la profesora
teddy el osito
telephone el teléfono
television la televisión
ten diez
thermometer el termómetro
thin delgado/delgada
thirteen trece
three tres
ticket el billete
ticket collector el revisor
tidy ordenado/ordenada
tiger el tigre
toilet el váter
tomato el tomate
tools las herramientas
toothbrush el cepillo de dientes
toothpaste la pasta de dientes
towel la toalla
town la ciudad
toy el juguete
toy train el trenecito de juguete
traffic lights el semáforo
train el tren
train driver la maquinista
travel el viaje
tree el árbol
trolley el carrito
trousers el pantalón
trunk el baúl
twelve doce
twenty veinte
two dos
ugly feo/fea
uncle el tío
van la furgoneta
vegetables las verduras
vehicles los vehículos
to walk andar
wardrobe el armario
washbasin el lavabo
water el agua
wave la ola
weather el tiempo
whale la ballena
wheelbarrow la carretilla
wheelchair la silla de ruedas
white blanco/blanca
wind el viento
window la ventana
witch la bruja
wood el tablón
wreck el naufragio
x-ray la radiografía
x-ray machine el detector de rayos x
yacht el yate
yellow amarillo/amarilla
zebra crossing el paso de cebra
zoo el zoo

Colours – Los colores

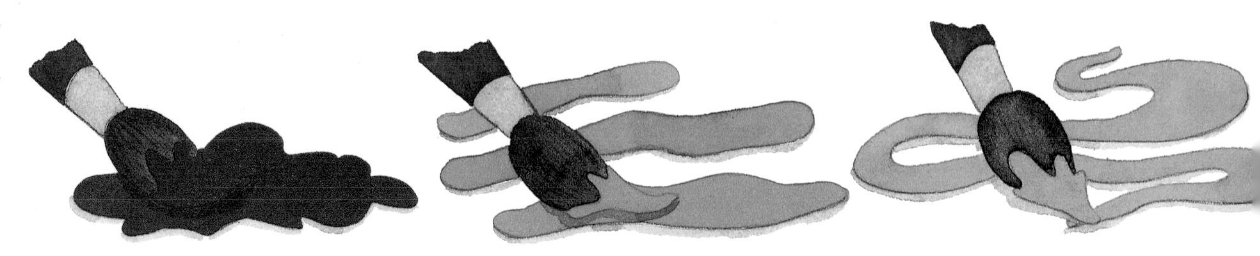

red
rojo/roja
ro-ho/ro-ha

blue
azul
athool

green
verde
bairdeh

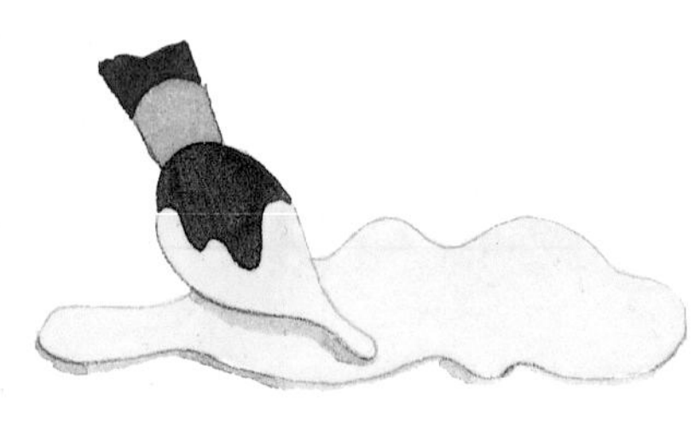

yellow
amarillo/amarilla
amaree-yo/amaree-ya

black
negro/negra
neggro/neggra

orange
naranja
naranha

white
blanco/blanca
blanko/blanka

purple
morado/morada
morah-do/morah-da

brown
marrón
marron